Love's Letters

A Collection of Timeless
Relationship Advice
from Today's Hottest
Marriage Experts

28 DAY DEVOTIONAL

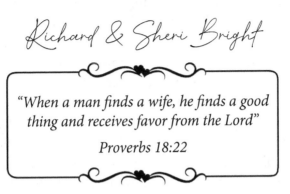

Richard & Sheri Bright

> "When a man finds a wife, he finds a good
> thing and receives favor from the Lord"
>
> *Proverbs 18:22*

Dear Determined Couple,

The struggle is real—the hurt is real—the pain is real.

Richard

My bride and I share this love letter to you as words of hope. Though we don't know your particular issues, rest assured you are not the only ones going through this tough season. It's "almost" a twisted rite of passage for couples. And because no one really talks about it, we're left to suffer in silence.

The mother of a dear pastor friend of mine said, "When you speak from your mind, you change people's minds, when you speak from your heart, you change people's hearts, but when you speak from your life, you change people's lives."

Sheri and I would love to change your lives and marriage.

We are a blended family, also known as the failures in some churches. They don't say it, but you feel it. You know, the ones who couldn't quite figure it out the first time. Or second. Sheri says we're a blender family because we were just thrown together without any working knowledge about marriage and what we were up against. Kids, exes, parents, dogs, and cats were just jammed into a blender and ground to a pulp. The failure and guilt we brought into this marriage, mixed with drugs, alcohol, and pornography, was a toxic setup for failure.

One of my favorite scriptures is Hosea 4:6: "My people perish from the lack of knowledge."

We were struggling just to stay alive, much less happy and whole. When we started out we hadn't a clue on how to avoid becoming another failed marriage statistic. As the husband and spiritual head of the family, I had no earthly idea how to untwist or make sense of my broken life, or the broken lives I'd helped create.

The good news is, God knows exactly how to untangle the worst mess. Another wonderful tidbit I learned was that I wasn't supposed to figure it all out by myself. God designed the covenant marriage so that I had a helper. My wife was always in my corner and ready to dig in, but it was me who had to first realize that we were indeed on the same team.

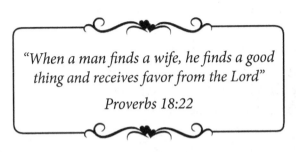

> *"When a man finds a wife, he finds a good thing and receives favor from the Lord"*
>
> *Proverbs 18:22*

My bride was not going to settle for the brokenness we shared daily, so she convinced me to try church, to try Jesus. I had so many issues with God I wasn't sure church was the right answer. But we started attending regularly, and I was shocked at what we found. The preconceived notions I had about what I called "religious people" were all wrong. It was an idea I'd set in my mind as a way of avoiding God and His people. I was also a little unsure of how to feel about the change in my thinking because I'd never felt genuine love from people who shared what we'd been struggling with—marriage.

I wish I could say by simply walking into a building that I was set free from all of the issues that had plagued me for most of my life, but the truth is, there is a process. Personally, it didn't take days or weeks or even months. Over the next few years, I continually walked in God's grace. I'd mess up, but quickly confess, apologize, and learn to continue moving toward the goal of being the man God created me to be and the husband my wife deserved. Through God's love I learned to love myself, and that allowed me to love my wife without limits. Instead of loving out of guilt because I'd caused pain, I was loving out of the abundance of love God first showed me. He wants to show you that very same love.

Sheri

In all honesty, my husband was starting to change for the better, but it was not fast enough for me. I'd been through the struggle, and all I wanted was peace in marriage. Richard would share that his heart was in a different place, but because I was expecting results, I didn't see the spiritual side of my husband. God was doing a work to him before He could do something wonderful through him.

Because love as I'd known it was performance based, it was hard to extend grace, mercy, and forgiveness to him. In my mind, he hadn't earned it. I wanted our marriage to succeed, and that desire was demanding things from Richard that he, in his spiritual transformation, hadn't yet experienced. The true change for both of us would only come as we continued to commit to surrounding ourselves with other believers who were able to mentor and model what healthy marriages looked like.

Simple, right? Well, the first

four years were like pulling teeth to get Richard and the kids to services. My commitment at the start was more about saving my marriage than serving God. I now understand that what mattered most wasn't what motivated us to be involved in a Bible-believing body of Christ, but that we were going. Once there, God's Word would take care of the rest.

> *"All things work together for good to them who love God"*
>
> *Romans 8:28*

And then one day my hubby opened up and started talking with me. We dove deep for the first time in our relationship. We started to pray every day with each other. Our lives were getting better, things started to turn around—to God be the glory! One Sunday, God told me to be real and transparent about our broken lives. That transparency forever changed our lives because God revealed a gift of comedy and teaching in us.

We want you to know that if God will grow us and turn a doomed marriage into something beautiful, then He will do it for you too. I wasn't afraid to speak up and be real about the shape of our marriage because we needed help desperately. After class everyone came up and thanked us for being honest and raw. That day, the ministry God gave us was born.

God wants you to be in love with each other and in love with Him. He is the only one who can bring life back to something dying. In this case, our marriage. We are praying for you and your relationship every day. Don't give up! Marriage is worth the fight. Expect to be in love again, expect to write each other love letters, expect the best from each other.

We declare that the love you once had will blossom, that seeds of success are being planted again. We declare that Jesus is the center of your lives. That you will reap the best of what life has to offer. That you will realize the lies the enemy has told you about your spouse. We declare that anything that comes against you is broken in Jesus's name. We believe mercy, grace, and forgiveness will run you down and overtake you. Do the world a favor, do yourself a favor, and fall in love again!

Love,
Richard and Sheri Bright

About Us

Richard and Sheri Bright are comedians and entertaining speakers helping couples put fun and inspiration back in their relationships. They share their humorous and transparent stories at churches, couples date night events and marriage conferences across the U.S.

https://www.brightermarriage.com

Hallee & Gregg Bridgeman

> "As the Father loved Me, I also have loved
> you; abide in My love."
>
> John 15:9

Dear Friends,

Hallee

I was a war bride. Gregg and I met as he prepared to deploy with the 20th Special Forces Group (Airborne) in 2002. We soon realized God had brought us together and that we would eventually marry. However, because of the danger he would soon face, we decided to marry right away so I would become his military dependent. That way, if something happened to him, the army would view me as his wife, which has a very different official status than a fiancée or girlfriend. It wasn't a traditional courtship or first year of marriage, but we had a plan to grow together as husband and wife, to create a firm foundation of the two of us reaching toward God. We prayed and read the wisdom gleaned from God's Word and knew that success depended upon our ability to always abide in each other.

Gregg

By our ninth year of marriage, Hallee and I had spent far more time separated than not. I spent most of my time in Afghanistan, though we met for short weeks in Kuwait and in the UAE on two occasions. That kind of distance and stress can—and has—broken countless marriages. Couples live separately with thousands of miles and dozens of time zones between them. We went into this time of separation, and others like it, intending to stay united as one—physically separated but together in spirit—by always abiding in each another.

Us

Abide is a verb. It takes action and intent. The Bible has a lot to say about abiding. In John 15, Jesus says: "As the Father loved Me, I also have loved you; abide in My love."

Jesus speaks to His disciples here, so this is not about a romance. However, so often, scripture compares Christ's loving relationship with the church to the loving relationship of holy matrimony and often describes abiding in that context. In fact, Christ uses the word *abide* eight times in this single chapter of John.

Translated from the Greek word *menō*, to *abide* is to remain as one, not to become another or different. This was our greatest desire, and it became our mission to remain as one, to abide in each other.

We videoconferenced when possible and emailed daily prayers to each other. We constantly spoke of the other, prayed for each other, and sent pictures and encouragement across the miles. In the end, with the years of separation finally over and our lives starting to look "normal," we'd passed our tenth anniversary and had grown into a strong couple. The time we spent separated by oceans and time zones hadn't pulled us apart.

Together today, the attitude of abiding is ingrained into our very nature. When we consider those years of our early marriage, our minds don't go to the distance and time spent apart as much as they go to the intimacy we enjoyed despite the physical separation. We two are one, a single unit, serving God with like-minded desires to further His kingdom and love our neighbors. Our family decisions are made together, as one. We make our personal choices in light of how individual decisions may impact us as a couple or our family as a whole.

Our love and appreciation for each other made the "forced" time together during the 2020 COVID-19 pandemic's quarantine a relief and a blessing to savor instead of a hardship to endure. We want to work together, share together, spend the days and nights together. Even though we are not separated, we are still actively abiding in each other every moment. We are as close now as we have always been.

When life separates you, it doesn't have to pull you apart. You can abide in each other as one and feel just as close as if you share the same bed at night and can make eye contact each morning.

We encourage you to embrace abiding in one another the same way Christ asked us to abide in Him. Remember your spouse as you pray, plan, and daily demonstrate a godly marriage for your children.

Pray for each other right now that God can unite you closer as a couple and teach you about His intention for abiding.

Yours in Christ,
Gregg and Hallee Bridgeman

About Us

With nearly a million book sales, Hallee Bridgeman is a best-selling Christian author who writes action-packed romantic suspense focusing on realistic characters who face real-world problems. Her work has been described as everything from refreshing to heart-stopping exciting and edgy.

https://www.halleebridgeman.com/biography

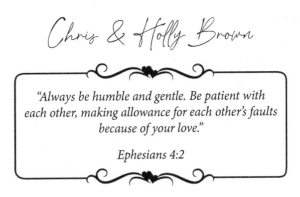

Chris & Holly Brown

"Always be humble and gentle. Be patient with each other, making allowance for each other's faults because of your love."

Ephesians 4:2

Dear Couple in a Difficult Season,

I sat there across from my husband in a white vinyl booth at the only open restaurant we could find at nine p.m in Seattle's Pike's Place Market. I couldn't taste the Chinese food at all and could barely swallow because of the lump in my throat. Anxiety had been winning for days. It took everything in me to make this trip and support Chris as he ministered to so many.

I was going through the emotions but trying to feel as little as possible. Actually, the only thing I wanted during that dinner was the wine. The wine would help calm me down. I took a sip of Chardonnay and forced it down around the lump. There was more going on inside of me that I hadn't told Chris, and

I was feeling anxious and disconnected from him because of it. But I loved him and if I told him everything, would I lose him? I couldn't risk that. The risk was too high...but living with anxiety, feeling uncovered and alone at all times was wearing on me.

I didn't want to live this way, but I was so afraid to open up about what was really going on in my own soul. Despite sincere efforts to hold it all in, a tear escaped without my permission and slid down my cheek. When Chris saw my tear...no, when he saw me and the pain behind my teary eyes, he said, "Come here. Come sit by me. I want to tell you something." I got up and moved next to him. He put his arm around me, looked me in the eyes, and said, "I love you. I love you with everything in me. Even if you told me the worst thing I could possibly imagine, I'm going to tell you that I love you. That I forgive you. I am still here and I will stay here by you. Forever. We will get through anything."

That day changed everything about our marriage. The day Chris led with forgiveness.

Chris and I want you to know that your marriage can survive this difficult season. In seasons like this, it becomes natural to retreat into your own self. To keep it all in and not let them know what's going on inside of you. It doesn't take long for all conversation to be only about the weather and the family schedule. The Bible tells us that one of the best things we do during these times is to gently and humbly lead with forgiveness.

Ephesians 4:2 says: "Always be humble and gentle. Be patient with each other, making allowance for each other's faults because of your love."

Maybe start the conversation with, "I want to know what is going on inside of you, and no matter what it is, I can handle it. We will get through it." When we lead this way, we let our spouse know we are safe, protective, and strong enough to handle who they really are. This draws out the depths of our partner's soul, the parts they think we could never handle. Most people rarely get the luxury of doing life alongside someone that can handle those parts of us and still deeply love us. To be fully seen and fully accepted is to be loved. Most people stay hidden because we fear the rejection of our spouse if we were fully seen. Sadly, most people never feel fully loved.

Don't be afraid of the difficult seasons in marriage. Your love grows deeper when you survive these times together. Have you considered how much more the beauty of a sunrise seems to take our breath away when we've survived an unbearable night? The same is true in marriage. Difficult seasons are a part of it, but beauty will come again. And when it does, you won't take for granted what it feels like to have your heart skip a beat when they lean in to kiss you.

These things will feel lost at times in marriage, but fight for your marriage, lead with forgiveness, and they will come again. And when the beauty comes again, if you led with forgiveness, this time it will be with someone who knows a little more of the depths of your soul. That is a level of intimacy that can only be built by traveling through seasons of good and difficult together. It is an intimacy not easily replaced. Protect it. Fight for it. Lead with forgiveness.

Love,
Chris and Holly Brown

About Us

Highly sought after Pastor, Speaker, and Church Leadership Expert, Chris brings over 20 years of ministry and financial experience. He worked alongside Dave Ramsey for years as a nationally syndicated radio host for "Life, Money, and Hope."

https://www.chrisbrownonair.com

Jody & Nan Burleen

Dear Couples in Need of Conversation,

"But you said you would..." "You always/never do..."
"Why do you..., when I have told you..."

Kind of sounds like conversations you'd have with
your kids, doesn't it? Yet, these are typical conversation
starters in our marriages with our spouses—our true
love, the one we vowed to do life with, best friend, and
lover. We expect that person to be a mind reader. After
all, they should know what we want, right? But is that
fair? Realistic? Successful? Do we want our marriage

conversations to sound like we are talking to a child, or for us to sound bossy or like a domineering authoritarian?

Christ says that our marriages are to be a symbol of Him and His love, the church, to the world. A representation of how much He loves us! And His sacrifice! (Ephesians 5:21–33)

We have often said that instead of saying we are "married," we should say we are "sacrificed" to our spouse, like Christ was for His church. Marriage defined is two people who live their lives trying to out-serve one another. In addition to sacrifice, it takes lots of practice, conversations, and a mind of Christ!

After thirty years of marriage, my wife and I have gotten pretty good at knowing each other and learning to adapt relatively quickly to our individual quirks. But that wasn't always the case. It's taken years and countless conversations (some civil and others not so civil) to get to where we are today. But in every case, it was talking it out that ended up with the desired result.

Way too often, couples get married and NEVER talk about issues that keep happening in their marriage. There is an assumed expectation that seems to never get resolved. For example (real life example): the wife wants her husband to pick up his clothes from the bedroom. But her expectation is not being met. Which makes her mad for what her husband thinks is "no reason."

Here is what happens. She

assumes her husband should know the expectation she has in mind—a clean room. But her husband, who is a slob, has a different expectation of what "clean" is.

Thus, neither expectation is being met, nor discussed. So, this vicious cycle of insanity continues, doing the same thing over and over and expecting different results. But once the wife discusses her expectation of a clean room, the "not so smart" husband begins to understand the frustration his wife has had over the years. Thus, once the expectation has been set, you both now have a gauge or a barometer, if you will, to see if the expectation is being met.

If the husband doesn't pick up his clothes, which happens often, the wife then can remind him of the expectation conversation you had about a clean room. The husband at that point has no excuse, and begins to meet his wife's expectation of a clean room. This example is a simple, but needed, conversation that couples must have and keep having. A clean room should be, and is, an easy conversation. The goal is to have tougher and more meaningful conversations and set the expectation in your home that will lead to a better understanding and appreciation for each other.

An expectation conversation is not just a talk! It's a time where spouses sit down and come up with a desired outcome that is beneficial for both parties. No matter the subject. And there needs to be give and take from both parties.

Expectation Conversations™—topics like sex, money, children, church, and faith—are topics many couples tend to avoid. Let us give you some "starter" ideas of the kind of conversations you need to have with each topic. (Please note: there are always concessions from both parties in every expectation conversation. It cannot be one sided. That is not a conversation, but instead a demand.)

♥ Sex—How Often? When? Where? Style?—Many couples live a frustrated sex life because they assume their spouse should know when they do and do not want to have sex, or how or where. Be honest with each other. Men, you can't expect it every day, and women, you can do it once a month. Again, this is a generalization, but you get the point.

♥ Money—Set up a budget...together. Tithe and hold each other accountable to the budget. Find out who is the spender and who is the saver. Work with each other to come up with a plan that works for both spouses.

♥ Children—How do you discipline? When do you discipline? What deserves a spanking and what deserves grounding? What roles do the father and mother play in each of these? There are a ton of parenting books out there; this is just an opportunity for you two to be unified. Don't let the kids divide the house.

♥ Church—Where do you go? How often? Where do you serve? Does it fit the kids and adults? Set the expectation of what you're looking for and find a church that you can raise your family in, serve, and fulfil the Great Commission.

♥ Faith—Where is your faith individually? As a couple? How can you grow together? What do you need to make that happen? Discipleship? Mentoring? Counseling?

Please know, these Expectation Conversations™ are meant to bring you closer together. Not further apart. If you get stuck on one of the questions/topics, take a break, bathe it in prayer, and come back to it at a later date. It's not a race to get them done, and don't tackle them all at one time. There may be years of hurts that need to be addressed first, or you are newlyweds and haven't ever stumbled onto some of these topics. Either way, just keep the conversations going, lean into the Lord, and remember, your spouse is not your enemy.

Love,
Pastor Jody and Nan Burkeen

About Us

Jody Burkeen is the founder and president of MAN UP! Gods Way Ministries. This ministry was birthed out of a desire to change the way Christian men "do" Christianity.

https://manupgodsway.org

Debra Clopton & Chuck Parks

"If you faint in the day of adversity, your
strength is small"

Proverbs 24:10

Dear Concerned Couple,

How do you have a happy marriage? Well, Debra and
I are certainly not experts on the subject, but we do have a
few thoughts we would like to share with you.

When we met twelve years ago, I had been through
a divorce and Debra's husband had passed away. We had
been through hard life storms in both of our lives, and
though it was tough, it made us stronger. What we had
been through helped us weed out a lot of the small
stuff that can affect a marriage negatively. So, what
helps us to have a happy marriage?

Don't sweat the small stuff! What is the small stuff?
In a marriage, the small stuff might be a disagreement
that neither one can remember why or how it got

started. Why let it steal your joy to begin with?

After we married, we were both set in our own ways. One day Debra folded the towels and put them in the bathroom cabinet. I went to get one and they were not folded the way I fold them. I quickly showed her how they needed to be folded. Well, she chuckled and informed me very quickly that she liked them folded how she did it. We laugh about it now and just fold the towels however we want to. It's really no big deal. But it can be if you let it.

This little incident early in our marriage helped us realize that we have our differences, but arguing over small stuff will never become bigger than our love for each other.

Then we have the big stuff. As we went, and continue to go, through adversity in our lives—as everyone will at some point—a lot of worldly things that used to be really important become insignificant.

James 1:2–4 says: "My brethren, count it all joy when you fall into various trials, knowing that the testing of your faith produces patience. But let patience have its perfect work, that you may be perfect and complete, lacking nothing."

One word that really stands out to us in this verse is the word *patience*. Tough times can teach us patience if we put our faith in God. God has stood with us through our adversity, and our faith has grown. We've become stronger, not weaker. We've learned to be more patient because we've learned to wait for God's timing, not *our* timing. Things that used to be high priority in our life have now become small stuff.

We started thinking about this devotional in September when Debra left to go to Hot Springs, Arkansas, with a couple of her girlfriends for a writing retreat. She was feeling good and excited. I was going to write my portion of this devotional during that time and she was going to add her part when she got home.

However, Debra started feeling bad two days into the trip. She was nauseated and had a low-grade fever. Wednesday was no better, so I drove five hours on Thursday and picked her up. We thought she might have COVID, so I drove another two hours to Texarkana and took her to Urgent Care to have her tested.

While filling out all the paperwork that's involved with a hospital visit, I looked at Debra and realized she wasn't able to write her name. Thirty minutes after getting inside the hospital she was having a seizure. My first thought was that she was having a stroke, and at that time, the thought of losing her was real.

Debra was diagnosed with viral encephalitis, and she spent five days in the ICU and another twenty-one days in the hospital. She has no memory of half of that time. It was a long journey, but we finally made it home and she's going to be fine. She's even started writing again. We give God all the glory for her healing. He was with us every step of the way.

This helped us realize how quickly we can lose someone we love—Debra already had lost a spouse, and now I thought I was losing Debra. All of a sudden, nothing else mattered—house, job, vacations—it all became small stuff. We realized that the big stuff, the important stuff, is our faith in God and each other, our family and friends.

If you want to have a happy marriage, don't sweat the small stuff and focus on the good stuff.

Love,
Chuck and Debra

About Us

A sixth-generation Texan, Debra lives on a ranch in Texas with her husband Chuck. She loves to travel and spend time with her family. She has written for Harlequin and Harper Collins Christian and now with DCP Publishing LLC. Since opening DCP Publishing LLC her books are selling worldwide and are regulars on the Top 100 list and Bestseller list in USA and around the world.

https://debraclopton.com

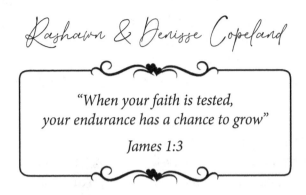

Rashawn & Denisse Copeland

> "When your faith is tested,
> your endurance has a chance to grow"
>
> *James 1:3*

Dear Tested Couple,

Trusting God Through the Test

Not long ago, my wife Denisse and I had a disagreement. We had agreed to go visit the Ozark State Park in Arkansas, but we couldn't agree on when would be the best time to visit the park. Back and forth we went. A pleasant day went sour. The time came when it was time for me to fellowship and meet with other ministers. I gave Denisse a quick *see you later*. "We'll deal with all of this later," I said.

But God stirred my heart up with the urgency to deal with it now. The walk to the ministry meeting was short and sweet. Maybe five minutes at the very most, but that is all it took for

God to stab my conscience with His Word. "Therefore, if you are offering your gift at the altar and there remember that your brother or sister has something against you, leave your gift there in front of the altar. First go and be reconciled to them; then come and offer your gift" (Matthew 5–23 NIV).

It was a test. Would you pout and doubt or apologize? Would you ignore the tension or take care of it? Before my meeting started, I ran back to Denisse, gave her a kiss on her forehead and apologized for my stubbornness, and asked for her forgiveness. Later that evening, we reached a decision on the perfect time to visit the Ozark State Park, prayed together, and the tension was gone and we both were at rest.

The worst thing you could do today is see your troubles as hassles and hurts. Through the lenses of that perspective births bitterness and anger. However, in contrast if you see your troubles as a test, used for God's glory and your spiritual growth, which is conforming you to the likeness of His Son Jesus, you'll pass every test with flying colors. "And we know that in all things God works for the good of those who love Him, who have been called according to His purpose" (Romans 8:28).

Thought to Ponder

Every day you can expect tests through people, pain, and problems that arise. Can you identify your test today? When was the last time you were tested?

At times our friends, family, or spouse can be the first ones to press our buttons. Maybe it's a co-worker or a professor? Acne or a toothache? A loaded work schedule that may have you anxious? Whatever it is or whoever they are, remember God is at work amid all your pain and problems. Amen!

Love,
Rashawn and Denisse

About Us

Hello! We are Rashawn and Denisse, and we are the founders of "Without Walls Ministries". We have a heavy heart stirred towards millennials to meet them in the midst of brokenness and lead them to the finished work of Jesus Christ.

https://www.copelandministries.org

Luke & Anna Cunningham

> "God blesses those who are merciful,
> for they will be shown mercy."
>
> Matthew 5:7

Dear "Opposites Attract" Couple,

Notice when the experts humorously use the phrase "opposites attract" they never say, "Opposites make great marriages." Wonder why? Because opposites can also attack! If you and your spouse find yourselves on the unhealthy end of the opposites, don't worry, there's still hope for your marriage. According to the enneagram, Anna and I are the worst possible matches for each other. Ten years, three kids, and a healthy marriage later, I'm thankful Jesus can transcend a personality number, though it wasn't always this way.

I like to plan. Plans are a limitation to Anna's creativity. I believe there's only one way to load the dishwasher. Anna believes as long as it lands inside the stainless steel box, we're good to go. Toilet paper should always roll off the top. She thinks I'm nuts. I'm early. She's… you get the point. Our disagreements always revolved around me being too harsh, rigid, and controlling, while she was carefree, selfish, and never prepared. At least that's what we said to each other. For a while, the enneagram was right. Fire meet gasoline. We were opposites who attacked!

Our differences became dividing lines. Each time one was crossed, we'd fight to get the other back in their rightful place. The turmoil reached a boiling point and we finally decided we needed to get some help. Several counseling sessions later we were starting to click, then we both experienced the "Ah-ha" moment that changed everything.

Our counselor said it casually, but it hit different! Ready? You're not going to like it, but you need to hear it. *You're just as difficult to love as your spouse.* "But she leaves the lights on every time we leave the house!" *You're just as difficult to love.* "But he gets annoyed when I don't want to strategically plan my shopping route when running into Target." *You're just as difficult to love.*

As this simple awareness began to settle into the framework of our marriage, new mercies for each other started uniting our hearts in a way we'd never experienced before. Mercy is God giving us what we don't deserve. Paul emphasizes

God's great mercy in Romans 5:8 by declaring, *"God showed His great love for us by sending Christ to die for us while we were still sinners."* It's easy to recognize our desperate need for mercy in our relationship with God. Seeing it in our marriages is a different story. Yet, Jesus extends this heart of mercy beyond our salvation to the daily encounters of our lives. He shares the hidden blessing of mercy in Matthew 5:7, *"God blesses those who are merciful, for they will be shown mercy."* The marriage translation: "Be merciful to your spouse. God has been merciful to you, and you've been just as difficult to love."

Opposites attract. Opposites attack. But opposites can also have a great marriage when the mercy of God triumphs over the annoyance of difference. Paul reminds us in Colossians 3:12 that because God chose to love us, we should clothe ourselves with mercy. Allow "I'm just as difficult to love as my spouse" to remind you of God's great mercy and inspire you to extend that mercy to your spouse, whether or not they deserve it.

How does embracing *I'm just as difficult to love as my spouse* change the way you view each other?

Love,
Luke and Anna

About Us

Pastor Luke and Anna are both from Kansas City but their kids are Texans so they consider themselves "part" Texan. Outside of the Kansas City Chiefs and sweet BBQ, they've integrated into living in the Lone Star State. Together, Luke and Anna are passionate about seeing people come to know, and come to grow in Jesus. Luke and Anna have three kids, Zion, Canaan, and Zadok. Their family motto is to, "Have fun and enjoy each other." This usually means family dates to Whataburger and swinging in the backyard, but can also include ice cream runs, wrestling matches on the living room floor, and family dance parties!

https://arkhuntsville.com

Ron & Cheryl Edmondson

> *"Above all, love each other deeply, because love covers over a multitude of sins."*
>
> *1 Peter 4:8 NIV*

Dear Best Friends,

When I shared with Cheryl we had been asked to write a devotional for a collective book to help other marriages, Cheryl quickly said our topic should be about building a lasting friendship in the marriage. We have made a lot of mistakes in marriage (and life), but I think we have done pretty well in this area.

As I thought about Cheryl's suggestion, my mind instantly went back to the days when we owned a business together. It was a small manufacturing company where we at times had as many as forty employees. (I always felt the weight of responsibility for the families represented by our employees.) I led the company in vision, sales, and production. Cheryl served as our accountant.

Unfortunately, we had cash flow issues throughout almost our entire ownership. I would go to the post office every morning praying the needed payments were in the mail.

Thankfully, we never missed a payroll or failed to pay our taxes, but I am certain some of our vendors would have appreciated being paid sooner. Cheryl often accused me of running past her office door because she was always looking for me to somehow bring more income to our business.

That was not the only stress in our lives at the time. I was also serving in an elected governmental office as a councilman and vice-mayor of our city. Cheryl was involved in leadership at the parent organizations of our boys' schools. And our two boys were each involved in sports activities. We were extremely involved with our church and I served on numerous boards in the community. It was a stressful season in our life—and frankly, in our marriage.

Looking back now, I can clearly see that our friendship with each other is what helped us weather those days. We never stopped being each other's best friend.

If Cheryl and I had any advice for couples in marriage, it would be to remain friends. That sounds cliche perhaps. You would almost assume that came naturally, but so many couples develop other interests beyond each other, which eventually divide them or even tear them apart. For example, when one spouse has a hobby not shared by the other spouse, eventually they are running in separate lanes. This does not mean the husband can't enjoy an occasional golf game with friends or the wife enjoy a shopping day with girlfriends, which are healthy too. But if every Saturday or day off is spent apart from each other, it will be harder to maintain the friendship.

One way Cheryl and I strive to maintain our friendship is with our schedule. When our boys were at home we purposefully planned frequent getaways together. As empty nesters, we call every Saturday our "date day." We walk together regularly. We both have busy lives, but regardless of the stress of the week, we know Saturday is coming. Of course, there are interruptions. We can't control what happens around us. Our aging parents need us more these days. We have grandchildren that might interrupt our plans. (And we seriously welcome that.) But to the best of our ability, we protect our time together. We see it as mission critical in maintaining the strength of our relationship and our friendship with each other.

I love the truth of Song of Solomon 3:4: "I have found the one whom my soul loves." After raising our children, working in our own business together, and serving in ministry together—we still feel that way about each other. We are thankful for our friendship.

Love,
Ron and Cheryl

About Us

Ron and Cheryl live in Nashville, Tennessee near their oldest son, his wife, and two granddaughters. They have another son, his wife, and another granddaughter. Both of their children are in full-time vocational ministry. Ron has been a pastor or ministry leader for almost 20 years, after a long career in the marketplace. Additionally, Ron served in an elected office and on dozens of nonprofit boards. Cheryl loves to invest relationally in younger women and marriages. Both Ron and Cheryl enjoy traveling, long walks, and simply being together. They advise all couples to maintain strong friendships throughout their parenting time - so they can better love their empty-nesting times.

https://ronedmondson.com

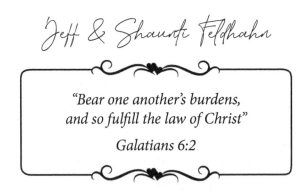

Jeff & Shaunti Feldhahn

> "Bear one another's burdens,
> and so fulfill the law of Christ"
>
> *Galatians 6:2*

Carry Your Spouse's Heart

Dear Frontline Couple,

You know that your spouse carries some unique burdens. One or both of you is a first responder, on the front lines. There is a lot riding on those shoulders. So in a manner very different from most couples, you are both having to think about safety, about how that stress is being handled, and how it is impacting the family, the kids, or your relationship. You intimately understand the need to, as the Bible puts it, "bear one another's burdens." And because you care about each other, you *want* to do that.

So we are going to let you in on a little secret: there is a much, much more fundamental burden that is running under the surface of your spouse than a worry about safety, time away from the kids, or "bringing the job home." Subconsciously, the person you are sharing your life with, whom you think you know so well, is burdened by *unseen vulnerabilities of the heart.* And over sixteen years of research, we've seen these vulnerabilities are probably very different from yours and thus very, very unseen by you. It will be life changing for both of you once you *see* those matters of the heart and treat them tenderly.

The key is this: although there are always exceptions, men and women *tend* to have two very different sets of primary self-doubts and insecurities.

Guys, believe it or not, that beautiful, competent woman you are married to probably has a very real question always running under the surface. "Am I lovable? Am I beautiful?" And crucially, that question *does not go away just because you got married.* It just morphs: "Is he glad he married me? Would he choose me all over again? Am I beautiful to *him?*"

These are subconscious questions, but they are so real. And when they are triggered, they rise up and circle in her heart until she is reassured.

Picture this scenario: things have been difficult at work and you have been distant or stressed. One morning you two have an emotional argument over breakfast, then, angry, you head out for your shift. As you drive up the road, you start thinking about work. So your thoughts about that argument switch off—and you hope the same thing happens in her.

It doesn't.

If she is like eight in ten women, her vulnerability has now been triggered. Worry rises up in her gut. She has the anxious feeling, "Are we okay?" And that worry will circle until she is reassured.

So how do you reassure her? What does it look like to bear this burden of her tender heart? In this case, stop before you leave and say something to reassure her. "Look, I'm angry and I need some space. But I want you to know: *we're okay.* I love you, and I'll text you later." Then text her later. Cop to whatever it is *you* handled wrong. And tell her again that you love her. By doing this, you will be loving her and carrying her vulnerable heart in a profound way.

Now, let's switch it.

Ladies, believe it or not, that strong, confident-looking man you are married to has a very real self-doubt always under the surface. Rather than, "Am I worthy to be loved for who I am on the inside?" a man's deep question is: "Am I able? Am I any good at what I do on the *outside?*" He wants to tackle a challenge and do great things; he wants to be a great husband and father and paramedic—but he feels like he has no idea how and is always messing up. It's a painful feeling in a way we can't quite grasp. There is so much insecurity that we don't even know is there!

Because that vulnerability is running under the surface, it can be triggered by small little negative messages we send. We come along behind him after he does the dishes and put them back in the dishwasher "the right way." We ask seemingly minor "why" questions: "Why did you put the kids in *those* clothes?! It's thirty degrees outside!" We roll our eyes, or tease him in front of his buddies about being unable to fix the leaky faucet. His vulnerable heart hears, "No, you're not able! No, you're not good at what you tried to do. In fact, you failed."

It is the most excruciating feeling imaginable. (And then, even worse, we think he is being *so oversensitive*.)

So what do you do? What does it look like to bear this burden of his tender heart? Stop yourself from correcting him (thereby sending him the "you're inadequate" message) unless it's so important that it is *worth* hurting his feelings. Look for ways to say "thank you" instead. "Thank you for doing the dishes, honey." (And then remind yourself it is more important to bear your husband's burdens than to have it done exactly the way *you* would!)

Because "thank you" is a man's version of "I love you," the simplest statement of appreciation is loaded with what his heart is longing to hear: "I noticed what you did… and it was *good*…and I appreciate it."

By doing this, you will be loving him and carrying his vulnerable heart in a profound way.

Friends, bear one another's burdens by learning the hidden things of your spouse's heart and speaking life to their area of secret vulnerability. By building our spouse up in this way, we are indeed "fulfilling the law of Christ." We are, as Jesus asks (John 13:34), working to "love one another as I have loved you."

With you on the journey,
Jeff and Shaunti Feldhahn

About Us

Jeff and Shaunti Feldhahn are social researchers, popular speakers, and best-selling authors. Their fascinating, groundbreaking books, such as *For Women Only, For Men Only*, and *The Kindness Challenge*, have sold more than 3 million copies in 25 languages and are used in homes, businesses and counseling centers worldwide. The latest language? Tigryana. They had to look it up! Jeff and Shaunti live in Atlanta with their two kids and two cats who think they are dogs. Connect with them on Instagram or Facebook (@shauntifeldhahn) or sign up for their blog at shaunti.com.

Debra & John Fileta

"Love...always protects"

1 Corinthians 13:4,7

Dear Couple Longing to Protect Your Marriage,

Anything of value is worth protecting. And marriage is certainly something of value. When John and I got married, the pastor took a circular-shaped block out of his pocket and reminded us of the importance of drawing a circle of protection around our marriage. That imagery has stayed with us for many years. To protect your marriage, you have to be deliberate about drawing a circle of boundaries, keeping it safe from within and protected from without.

No one wakes up and says, "I think I'm going to destroy my marriage today." Major relationship problems usually begin with small steps. But little by little, a marriage with no boundaries can become a breeding ground for heartbreak and pain.

Over the course of my career as a licensed counselor observing marriages, as well as in our own personal life, my husband and I have observed three specific areas in marriage that tend to be problem spots if we aren't being deliberate to protect them. We want to share them with you:

1. Misplaced Emotions: Sharing your deepest feelings with people other than your spouse is an area in which you need to be cautious. Your spouse should always come first. And if you do find yourself sharing with others, you should always ask yourself this: is this person part of the solution? If the answer is no, and you haven't yet shared with your spouse, you're likely crossing the boundary of misplaced emotions.

2. Private Interactions: There's no one-size-fits-all way to set a boundary around your interactions, but the key is to always be transparent with your spouse when you're interacting with the opposite sex. John and I are a team, and we go above and beyond to include or inform each other in every interaction that involves someone of the opposite sex. We share our

passwords, loop each other into emails, and share all the details with one another. Because a person who has nothing to hide becomes a safe place for their spouse to hide their heart.

3. Wasted Time: With busy schedules, crazy lives, and the lure of technology and social media, you can easily find your time slipping away. Two people can be in the same room, both on their phones or devices, not spending any time with one another at all. It's important for us to prioritize where we allow our time to go, or we find ourselves exchanging the intimate for the inanimate. Don't allow the "water" of your time and attention to be poured out to others, all while your marriage is dying of thirst. Protecting our time means setting limits with how we will spend our time, and who we will invest it in.

Everything of value is worth protecting, and my dear friends, your marriage is one of the most valuable things you'll ever be given. So, in all our actions, behaviors, and interactions—let us choose to protect our marriage.

Reflection: Together as a couple, take some time to discuss these three areas and the specific boundaries you have set/will set to protect your marriage for each one. Do you need to set any additional boundaries? Talk through this, and then write out your boundaries together.

Love,
Debra and John

About Us

Debra and John Fileta live in Lancaster, PA, with their four children. Together, they run the relationship advice blog (TrueLoveDates.com) and relationship podcast (Love + Relationships) reaching millions of people with the message of healthy relationship. As a licensed counselor specializing in relationships, Debra is also the author of the books *True Love Dates, Choosing Marriage, Love In Every Season*, and *Are You Really OK?*

Connect with their ministry on Facebook
or Instagram @TrueLoveDates.

https://truelovedates.com

Kellie & Allen Gilbert

> "As a shepherd cares for his herd...so will I care for My sheep and will deliver them from all the places to which they were scattered."
>
> Ezekiel 34:12

Dear Lonely Couple:

Allen

Kellie and I met over forty years ago in a tiny country western bar. The Hi-Ho was a favorite hang-out for me and my skydiving buddies. We'd spend weekends jumping out of airplanes and then head over to the nearby bar for some cheap beers, usually staying until the place closed down.

I saw Kellie at a table with a bunch of girls and thought she was pretty cute. Even sitting, I could tell she looked good in a pair of jeans and asked her to dance. I soon learned Kellie wasn't like most of the girls I'd dated. She worked in the State Capitol Building as a governor's intern, and she'd bought her own home. I discovered her family owned a big ranch near Sun Valley—a ranch with a duck-hunting lake and hunting rights.

I was immediately all in. Oh, and I liked her too.

Kellie

Allen was nothing like the boys I'd dated before. He reminded me of some of the characters I'd read in romance novels—you know the type: the bad boy with an amazing heart.

Our first real date was at a mountain lake resort in central Idaho over the Fourth of July. Allen was scheduled to do an exhibition jump. While he went up, I stayed behind with others in our group on the deck of the Yacht Club and watched. I was fascinated as the skydivers made these amazing formations in the sky. Allen had thousands of jumps under his belt, had just returned from a tour in Europe with a bunch of skydivers, and was well known in those circles as the one of the best around. Minutes later, that proved out as other jumpers landed in the road, in the parking lot, one even in the lake. Allen, however, landed right next to where I was sitting. As his parachute floated gently to the floor of the deck, he picked my drink up off the table and said "Hey, babe. What are you doing for the rest of your life?"

Looking back, I was a goner at that moment! I was done with boring. Allen's life was filled with fun and adventure. I packed my bags and decided to go with him.

Unfortunately, we soon learned not all baggage is Gucci.

Allen

Our early married years were not free of difficulty, but they were good years. Kellie and I became Christians. To everyone who knew us, we were a happy couple. But, as time passed, we accumulated hurts and resentments. We became roommates. We never shared our feelings, never made plans or dreamed together. We slept on opposite sides of a huge king-sized bed and politely took turns in the bathroom.

Except for a few occasions, we didn't fight. But, we didn't connect much either. We simply marched through the years with our hearts filling with building resentment. Resentment can be fatal to the oneness God intended in a marriage.

Kellie

I was terribly lonely, and I think Allen was too. We both desperately wanted to get off the un-merry go 'round. What attracted me to Allen when dating, annoyed the Pete out of me after we were married. Likely, he could say the same. Unfortunately, we didn't have the tools to maneuver our differences. As a result, we spent years fighting with our silence.

Satan used that vulnerability to throw fuel on the dying embers of our marriage. He intended to destroy what we had built together.

Allen

We'd been married nearly forty years before we stepped out of our comfort zone and attended a marriage class through our church. There, we learned God had a lot to say about marriage. I learned how to honestly love my wife…how to honor God by honoring her. We both learned communication skills that allowed us to forgive each other for the disappointments and hurts. We started having date nights. We became friends again.

Kellie

A faithful God stepped in and fixed what we couldn't in our human strength.

I now strive to hug more and nag less. I try to make Allen feel respected, important, valued. I see him working to make me feel loved and secure. By following God's plan, we fell back in love.

Our marriage is living proof that Jesus is the good shepherd who comes after his lost sheep... and sometimes, He carries those of us with broken legs until we learn to walk again.

Love,
Allen and Kellie

About Us

Kellie Coates Gilbert has won readers' hearts with her compelling and highly emotional stories about women and the relationships that define their lives. A former legal investigator, she is especially known for keeping readers turning pages and creating nuanced characters who seem real.

In addition to garnering hundreds of five-star reader reviews on Amazon and other retail sites, Kellie has been described by RT Book Reviews as a "deft, crisp storyteller." Her books were featured as Barnes & Noble Top Shelf Picks and were included on Library Journal's Best Book List of 2014.

Born and raised near Sun Valley, Idaho, Kellie now lives with her husband of over thirty-five years in Dallas, where she spends most days by her pool drinking sweet tea and writing the stories of her heart. Together, Allen and Kellie serve as leaders in the marriage ministry at their church.

George & Tondra Gregory

> "Do not conform any longer to the pattern
> of this world, but be transformed by the
> renewing of your mind…"
>
> Romans 12:2

Dear Newlyweds,

When you get married, you look at that handsome hunk or that beautiful queen and think God has finally sent me the perfect ten to fulfill my dreams. In your eyes, they are the perfect ten. However, you married a lot more than what you see in front of you or on the surface. Your spouse brings with them a set of past experiences and circumstances which have shaped them in ways that even they may not understand totally. We call these circumstances "baggage." Everyone has baggage, whether seen or unseen, that can weigh on any marriage or relationship over time.

Unpacking your baggage is an essential part of laying a solid foundation to build a lifelong and healthy relationship. Your past can influence your behavior, your emotions, your opinions, as well as your convictions and expectations, unknowingly. Our backgrounds, past hurts, wounds, and experiences can become the unconscious filter through which you view yourself, your spouse, and your relationship. Oftentimes, this affects the lens in which you view your spouse's words and actions, which may be distorted.

Baggage may drive you to be more reactive and less objective in your interactions with each other. Therefore, making sure you understand and become aware of how your two worlds combine is essential to prevent an emotional collision in the future. The impact your past has on your present, as well as your future, must not be minimized, but rather understood and planned for.

Oh boy, did our individual pasts collide on an emotional level during our first few years of marriage! Tondra was raised in a single-parent household by her mother, and I was raised in a traditional two-parent household where my dad was the dominant voice while my mother was less vocal. Can you see where this is going? We were gasoline and fire. We both came into the marriage with unconscious expectations and beliefs about how to run and who ran things in our house.

Tondra thought she was in charge and had strong opinions. After all, in her mind that's what strong women did. I, on the other hand, thought I was in charge as I wanted to model my dad's strong leadership. Needless to say the unconscious, unspoken power struggle began just a few months into our marriage, leaving us feeling confused, frustrated, and at a loss as to why we could not get along. Our "happily ever after" was soon tested with each of us feeling unappreciated and unloved.

It wasn't until we slowed things down and started to deeply introspect that we were able to verbalize how things in our past shaped our views of ourselves, our roles, and communication styles. We even had to go through marriage counseling and mentorship. It helped us to see how our past lives were colliding in our present and keeping us from the future we desired. No matter how much you love each other, the key to figuring out how to make your marriage work begins with an awareness and understanding of your past.

Throughout our twenty-five years of marriage we have learned to intentionally identify our baggage from the past. The habitual pattern of many couples is to walk in avoidance or denial of how the past can impact their marriage. But God's Word is clear, "Do not conform any longer to the

told Ezekiel to begin declaring life over those dry bones he saw. All of the sudden the bones began to rattle in response to Ezekiel's life-giving words. Eventually, there was a fully assembled army that marched out of that valley full of hope, life, and ready to take on the world!

We want to encourage you that regardless of how you feel right now, make the decision to begin declaring, out of your mouth, life over you, your spouse, and your marriage. Even though things may feel dry and dead in your relationship right now, God can begin watering your small seed of faith. Just a simple act of declaring life over your marriage can spark the miracle of healing in your relationship.

In the darkest days of our marriage, we did not feel like declaring life over our relationship, but we made a choice to do it. We were disconnected, dry, and wishing for help but too embarrassed to ask for it. We started small. We started with phrases like, "Father, heal our marriage." "God, we put you at the center of our relationship." "We declare blessings over our marriage!" It didn't happen overnight, but every day we would declare life. Each day God would meet us with His undeserved grace and take us by the hand to lead us one step closer to the mountaintop.

Our challenge to you is this, look up! Don't focus on where you are, focus on where you're heading. Remember that your spouse isn't your enemy, Satan is, and your spouse isn't your savior. God is your savior! He has promised that He will never leave you alone regardless of how you might feel. Begin declaring life over your spouse and your marriage. Realize that you and your spouse are on the same team. We dare you to begin praying together! Pray blessings over each other. Read marriage books together. Proverbs 24:3–4 says that your house needs to be built on wisdom, knowledge, and understanding. Take the time to invest in your relationship by gaining that wisdom, knowledge, and understanding through books, date nights, counseling, and marriage classes. We believe that if God can do it for us, He can do it for you! Choose today to take the first step out of the valley!

Love,
Clayton and Ashlee

About Us

Clayton and Ashlee Hurst currently serve as the Marriage Pastors at Lakewood Church in Houston, Texas, under the leadership of Senior Pastor Joel Osteen. For years they struggled in a hopeless marriage until they humbled themselves and sought the help they needed. They don't have a perfect marriage, but today they have a strong marriage and a passion to help others. Clayton and Ashlee have been married over 24 years, have 3 children, and are authors of *Hope For Your Marriage*.

https://lakewoodchurch.com/marriage

Scott & Katie LaPierre

> "But the fruit of the Spirit is love, joy, peace, forbearance, kindness, goodness, faithfulness, gentleness and self-control. Against such things there is no law."
>
> Galatians 5:22-23

Dear Preparing Couple,

A Husband Gets the Wife He Prepares for Himself

Ephesians 5:26–27 says that Jesus: "might sanctify and cleanse her with the washing of water by the word, that He might present her to Himself a glorious church, not having spot or wrinkle or any such thing, but that she should be holy and without blemish." There is a tremendous truth contained in these words. Christ does what He does—sanctifying and cleansing the church—so that He can obtain for Himself a glorious church (or bride), one that has no spot or wrinkle, but is holy and without blemish. Here is the simplest way to sum it all up: *Christ gets the church He prepares for Himself.*

Since this is a picture for husbands and wives, what is the apostle Paul implying by this truth? Just as Jesus gets the church He prepares for Himself, a husband generally gets the wife he prepares for himself. Wives respond well to love, holiness, and obedience to God's Word. When a husband treats his wife forgivingly, lovingly, and tenderly, he will generally receive a more forgiving, loving, and tender wife. When a husband treats his wife unforgivingly, unlovingly, and harshly, he will generally find himself with a wife who is less forgiving, loving, and tender.

So aside from the fact that God commands a husband to take his wife to church, read the Word with her, pray with her, and help her grow spiritually, another great reason for him to do so is that he will receive a more spiritually mature wife. What kind of qualities will be produced as a result? Galatians 5:22–23 gives the answer: "The fruit of the Spirit is love, joy, peace, longsuffering, kindness, goodness, faithfulness, gentleness, self-control."

Conversely, husbands who do not lead their wives spiritually are likely to receive wives who are less spiritual. What is the opposite of that which is spiritual? The flesh: "Walk in the Spirit, and you shall not fulfill the lust of the flesh. For the flesh lusts against the Spirit, and the Spirit against the flesh; and these are contrary to one another" (Galatians 5:16–17). Verses 19–22 go on to list the "works of the flesh" that are manifest in a person who is not walking in the Spirit: hatred, contentions, jealousies, outbursts of wrath, selfish ambitions, dissensions, envy, even adultery.

How many husbands see these behaviors in their wives because they have been poor spiritual leaders? How many wives might be more spiritually mature if their husbands were nurturing them spiritually, praying for them, and reading the Bible with them? Tragically, I have heard some husbands talk terribly about their wives without considering the fact they may have received the wives they have prepared for themselves. Men have come into my office and told me how badly their wives act, only to make themselves look bad. I'm listening and thinking, *Would your wife be acting this way if you had been sanctifying and cleansing her as God's Word commands? It sounds like you may have gotten the wife you prepared for yourself.*

Galatians 6:7 tells us, "Do not be deceived, God is not mocked; for whatever a man sows, that he will also reap." While it's true that the context of this verse has to do with giving to the church, the principle also applies to a husband's relationship with his wife. Husbands generally reap what they sow in marriage. When husbands invest in their wives by sowing seeds of love and interest—

when they plant spiritual seeds of sanctification—they will reap what they've sown.

Let's summarize what we've learned by keeping these two truths in mind:

1. Husbands should contribute to sanctifying and cleansing their wives. God has commanded this and will hold husbands accountable for whether they fulfill this calling.

2. Husbands are to love their wives and lead them well so that they receive loving, sanctified wives. The good news is that God's command to husbands benefits them as much as it benefits their wives. A husband who loves his wife as God commands will bring great blessings to himself.

Love,
Scott and Katie

About Us

Scott LaPierre is a senior pastor, author, and conference speaker. He and his wife, Katie, grew up together in northern California, and God has blessed them with eight children they homeschool. You can learn more about Scott, his books, podcast, and speaking information on his website:

https://www.scottlapierre.org

Amber & Guy Lia

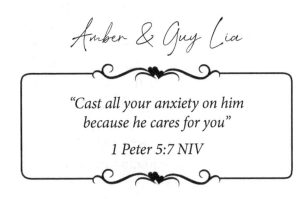

> *"Cast all your anxiety on him*
> *because he cares for you"*
>
> *1 Peter 5:7 NIV*

Dear Stressed-Out Couple,

It feels like too much, doesn't it? Adulting is hard. We understand. Life is tough at times.

As a couple, our own marriage has weathered rocky times with sick children, moving to new towns, job losses, and dreams that never saw the light of day. Whenever one of us began to feel the weight of stress, the other would often be the voice of reason. We encourage you to be one another's soft place to land, an anchor for one another in the storms of life.

Some of the hardest times in our own marriage were the seasons where we forgot we were a team. The times we tried to muscle through, *problem solving* instead of *promise keeping.* We committed for better or worse, right? Sickness and health? Good times and bad? Stress is not your enemy. *It's your opportunity.* It's your opportunity to show your spouse that you meant what you said at the altar. You would love him. You would cherish her. For better or worse—in times of stress and times of rich blessing. All of it! Together.

When stress hits, emotions run high. We snap at one another and become easily irritated. Seemingly small issues turn from mole hills into mountains, but we want to encourage you to be intentional to release it when you feel the stress mounting. Get ahead of it before it gets to your head!

Take a walk around the block, practice deep breaths, focus on the fact that your spouse is your ally, not your punching bag. You can choose to hold on to stress or release it in a healthy way.

An ever-present help in trouble, God beckons us to lay our fears, worries, and troubles at His feet:

"Cast all your anxiety on him because he cares for you" (1 Peter 5:7 NIV).

What would that feel like? Even now, as you read those words, do you sense the burden lifting? The Lord is far more able to handle your problems than you are. Let Him! In faith, give them to Him and have hope that everything will work out for your good, as God promises.

You love your spouse and they love you. That's why you chose one another in the first place! Allow your burdens to bring you together, not wedge you apart. You see, it's easy to carry your burdens alone, not wanting to saddle your worries onto your spouse, but when we became man and wife, we became *one*. Our hearts are knitted in the union of marriage, making us better *together*. Don't retreat from one another when times get tough. Slow down, breathe, and take the time to communicate and pray with each other. These stressful days are simply a vehicle for further intimacy.

Your stress can actually serve you, if you let it.

Rise above the flood of emotions and negative thinking, friend. Let it buoy you toward hope instead of despair. Release the stress to God. Draw close to your spouse. Remember God's promises to carry your burdens and see you through. It's an opportunity for intimacy and encouragement in your marriage, not an obstacle to claw your way through. Your story isn't this moment. But what a beautiful chapter it can be, when you invite God to use your stress to bless.

Much love and peace to you both,
Amber and Guy Lia

About Us

A former high school English teacher, Amber Lia is a work-at-home mom of four little boys. She is the bestselling coauthor of *Triggers: Exchanging Parents' Angry Reactions for Gentle Biblical Responses* and *Parenting Scripts: When What You're Saying Isn't Working, say Something New.* She and her husband Guy own Storehouse Media Group, a faith-friendly and family-friendly TV and film production company in Los Angeles, California. When she's not building sand castles with her boys on the beach, or searching for Nerf darts all over her house, you can find Amber writing to encourage families on her blog at MotherofKnights.com.

Guy Lia lives in Los Angeles, California, with his wife of fifteen years, Amber Lia, and their four boys, black lab, and two cats. A former TV development executive, Guy is now the co-owner of the values-based, family and faith friendly TV and film production company, Storehouse Media Group, and he is the cowriter of the book, *Marriage Triggers: Exchanging Spouses Angry Reactions with Gentle Biblical Responses.*

Shawn & Tricia Lovejoy

> *"Be devoted to one another in love.*
> *Honor one another above yourselves"*
>
> *Romans 12:10*

Dear Encouraging Couple,

The Power of an Encouraging Spouse

Have you ever stopped to think about what your husband faces in a typical day? No matter what his job is, he deals with demands, pressures, and probably a competitive drive that pushes him to constantly be better, do more, or measure up to some standard. In the midst of those demands and pressures from his career, he might even deal with pressures he places on himself to provide for his family, to be the dad he ought to be, or to keep his wife happy. I know sometimes our husbands seem like their minds are a million miles away, but I assure you these concerns weigh heavily on their hearts.

What about you, men? Did you know that your wife faces similar burdens?

She constantly tries to be all things to all people—an admirable, albeit impossible, goal. She longs to be a wonderful mother, but privately deals with guilt when she feels she's blown it. She feels pressure to say yes to everyone in her life and will exhaust herself trying to help others. She wants to be a team player and offer her best, even as she faces the unspoken fear that she'll be taken for granted. She is driven to lead well at work and home and will sacrifice her own rest to achieve significance. Husbands, your wives want to be loved for all they do. I assure you that love is the grand prize they are seeking.

With goals and demands weighing heavily on both sides of the gender gap, it's fair to assume that we could all use some encouragement…some recognition…some love. How could we partner together to help one another?

In scripture, Jesus taught that we should treat others the way we want to be treated. So, if encouragement and love would build you up, what would it do for your spouse? More than anyone else, our spouse needs to hear us say things like, "I'm with you no matter what," or, "I know you the best, and I love you the most." They need us to keep them focused on living out God's purpose for their lives not on the voice of the naysayers. Our encouragement means more to them than a thousand pats on the back by well-meaning friends. We have a voice of power in our spouses' lives. Let's leverage that voice to build them up!

How could you encourage your spouse today? Could you write a love letter? Could you tell him how much he impresses you? Could you thank her for all she does to provide for your family? Could you plan a celebration for one of her accomplishments? Could you compliment him in front of others? The ideas are endless.

Seize the opportunity to tell your spouse just how wonderful they really are. After all, our lives shouldn't be about us—about what we can get or what we want. Ultimately, our lives should be about what we can give— the love we can share—and the influence we have over the people closest to us. That's real love.

Love,
Shawn and Tricia

About Us

Shawn is the Founder & CEO of CourageToLead.com. His heart beats for coaching leaders through what keeps them up at night. Shawn has been a successful real estate developer, church planter, megachurch pastor, and successful entrepreneur and leadership coach. CourageToLead.com facilitates leadership growth and organizational health for leaders all around the globe.

https://www.couragetolead.com

Adam & Jami McCain

> *Two are better than one, because they have a good return for their labor: If either of them falls down, one can help the other up. But pity anyone who falls and has no one to help them up. Also, if two lie down together, they will keep warm. But how can one keep warm alone? Though one may be overpowered, two can defend themselves. A cord of three strands is not quickly broken.*
>
> *Ecclesiastes 4:9-12*

Dear Beautiful Couple,

God put you together…on purpose! Just like you chose each other, no matter if it was days, months, or years ago, the Creator of the Universe chose you… both of you! Or as we say it down South, chose y'all for His beautiful story! In the book of Ephesians, Paul reminds us that before the world was even created, we were on His mind, part of His Plan to redeem this earth…part of His Purpose!

One of the key elements we have found to a strong, lasting marriage is a shared purpose. In this hectic world we live in, many couples can feel like they are on parallel roads, or even living in parallel universes. The days can drone on as each goes off to execute their expected tasks...carpool, taxes, board meetings and household tasks. And if by chance the opportunity to do something more, something they feel they were born to do, occurs, those moments exist outside of the marriage: a promotion at work, a master's degree earned, or a great day on the golf course. Although there's nothing inherently wrong with any of these things, they can sometimes miss the mark for the reasons we were really placed on this earth. And in running down those separate paths, many times we're pulled apart instead of pulling up toward the person who captured our hearts.

But what if we stopped for a moment and asked the Lord what He dreams for us as a couple. For the both of us together. Could it be He has something very special in store? Ecclesiastes 4:9–12 talks about the power of two instead of one. The first thing it says is they have a "good return on their work." What does this mean? It means that whatever you hoped to leave as a legacy, when you realize the legacy is actually yours together, the return is exponentially greater. Later it says that same bond, with Jesus in the middle, a "three-strand" cord, is not easily broken. It's the glue that bonds through the tough times.

So when things get tense, and life doesn't add up, remember that the same God who placed the stars and planets in the heavens placed the two of you together for a reason. And not just to combine incomes to pay the bills or have a nice house, but because He knew that there is something that can only be accomplished when you come together with a shared purpose.

Our prayer is that you find yours!

Love,
Adam and Jami McCain

About Us

Adam McCain has been in full time ministry since the age of 19. He is known to many, not only for his years of service as Director of Christ for the Nations, but also as a spiritual father to ministers all over the world. In 2004, Adam and Jami established Global Youth Net, a missions organization that exists to raise up and equip a younger generation. Adam serves as the Lead Pastor of Hill City Church in Cedar Hill, TX where he resides with his wife, Jami, and their three children.

https://www.adammccain.org

Joshua & Keesha Melancon

> *"Be kind to each other, tenderhearted, forgiving one another, just as God through Christ has forgiven you"*
>
> *Ephesians 4:32*

Dear Couple with Issues,

Keesha and I write this to you today with compassion and understanding for your struggle. We have been there too. We'd like to tell you that we've gotten past all the issues that cause arguments and strife in our marriage to the place that we no longer argue at all, but that would be a lie.

So where is the hope in that last statement? Just hold on, some good news is coming.

All married couples generally have the same argument, just dressed in a different scenario. It can be so tiring and can drain the love and devotion you have for each other until there is nothing left but animosity toward each other.

Now the Bible tells us a few things, one of which is "Be kind to each other, tenderhearted, forgiving one another, just as God through Christ has forgiven you" (Ephesians 4:32). And we want to shoot back with, "Easy for God to say! Christ never got married. Lucky guy!" Right?

But here's the kicker. Marriage is hard. Let us say, "Amen." Or "Oh, me." Whichever fits.

What then is there to do?

Well, it will take some work, but the best things always do. Something important to understand is when under stress, any unresolved hurts from our past are argument magnets. Here's what we have learned and put into practice. We think it will help you as well.

First, an example of what can happen. We were going to change our names, but in the interest of you seeing right through that...

Keesha has a full and eventful day. I have also had an eventful day. We are pastors, so we have plenty of those.

I come home wanting some peace and quiet. I'm all talked out and don't want to process another thing. Neither does she. But she is also looking for that gallon of milk I promised to bring home... What starts with the "Where's the milk?" question ends with a "You never listen to me" statement. *What?*

What's more important? The milk? Or knowing I appreciate her, value her, and know how hard she works to make a great home and all that she does to co-pastor beside me? Feelings of being disconnected and unappreciated were the root here. Note: I can hop back in the car and go to the store, so I do.

Those types of things are rare now. Why? Do we experience less stressful days? Um, that would be a hard no. But we've learned to communicate to each other who we are. We are vulnerable with each other. We dig out the real issues we have through meaningful and consistent conversation.

What exactly does that look like?

Choose a time each day where you patiently catch up. It doesn't have to be hours. Could be sharing over a cup of coffee in the morning or a lunch date, or even a cup of tea in the evening will do. Or it might be an evening walk.

These times allow for unresolved or unprocessed feelings to be expressed and heard. It gives a more accurate portrait of the other's heart. It says, "I care enough to make time, give effort, and invest in you."

Also, you can use this time to have a bit of fun and focus more energy on each other's strengths, not weaknesses.

Another thing is to ask God to search your hearts for any resentment or bitterness that is residual from the pain of doing life intimately with another for a long period of time.

Sometimes what is revealed is that the issue is between you and God, not you and your spouse. You may have brought issues from another relationship, whether familial or dating, into your marriage, and your spouse is paying the price.

Be prepared to let God work on you. When you do you may find that "issue" with your spouse disappears as well. Allow God to wipe away with His mercy what He reveals. Extend mercy to others and include yourselves in that practice.

Bringing God into the equation is key to success. Every time. In everything. Even marriage. Especially marriage.

My wife and I are miles away from perfect, and yet still enjoy being married and the life that God has given. These tools we write here, though counter to the culture, keep us connected and living in the freedom and peace God has for all marriages. Including yours.

Make time for God and each other. It will change your life and your marriage. Jesus is just a prayer away. May the riches of God's blessing be upon your marriage.

Love,
Joshua and Keesha

About Us

Josh and Keesha are lead pastors of House of Prayer, a thriving church in south Louisiana. These former schoolteachers, he middle school, and she kindergarten, middle, and high school, are now passionate about and devoted to seeing people live whole healthy, and productive faith-filled lives.

A self-proclaimed church brat, Josh is the author of *Church Junkies: A pastor's perspective on what true spiritual health looks like, how to get it, and how to keep it.* Keesha centers her time on family, caring for the next generation of leaders, and ministering to women using community groups and one-on-one counseling. They reside in a small Louisiana college town and have two children. Look for them on Facebook @pastorjoshmelancon and @houseofprayer.

Jamal & Natasha Miller

> *"The Spirit of the Lord is on me, because he has anointed me to proclaim good news to the poor. He has sent me to proclaim freedom for the prisoners and recovery of sight for the blind, to set the oppressed free."*
>
> *Luke 4:18*

Anointed Marriage

Dear Anointed Couple,

Jesus states in Luke 4:18, "The Spirit of the Lord is upon me, He has ANOINTED me to preach the gospel, heal the brokenhearted, to preach deliverance to the captives, and the blind will see, and the oppressed will be set free" (NLT).

We come into marriage with each having our own preconceived ideas of what a successful and thriving marriage looks like…

Maybe it's that we get along great with very few arguments, we support one another in our careers, or maybe it's that we still go out on dates and have fun together…The list could go on depending on what you value most out of relationships. The question we would like to propose to you today is: do you know what an anointed marriage looks like?

In the book of Genesis, we see God make a very bold statement to Adam: "It is not good for man to be alone." This statement comes right after God shares His vision for man's responsibility on the earth: "Be fruitful and multiply. Fill the earth and govern it." This gives us insight into what makes a marriage an anointed marriage. It's when two people desire to partner with God to fulfill a mission that is bigger than them.

My wife and I have magnanimous goals we believe God has given us as a couple to accomplish. After getting married we discussed our passions and goals in order to better understand why God brought us together, and to be able to push each other to achieve them. Many couples marry without truly having the discussion of "Why did God bring us together?" Yes, to love one another, but also to love one another to action. That action involves fulfilling the purpose of God for your life. We knew that, if our goals were accomplishable on our own, then they weren't big enough.

We set goals that require God's empowering in order to accomplish them.

That empowering in the Bible is called "the anointing." The anointing is God's presence empowering you by way of the Holy Spirit.

We find in Luke 4:18, Jesus is ANOINTED, which means empowered by the Spirit of God to do specific things. God has called you and your spouse to dream big dreams, and to accomplish much for His glory. It is with the empowerment of God's anointing that you will do those things. A godly marriage must have the anointing to see the plan of God fulfilled in your lives.

Love,
Jamal and Natasha

About Us

It is our mission to see Married and Young increase the marriage rate and decrease the divorce rate in the World by helping singles, courting, engaged, and newly married couples establish a solid foundation for a successful Godly marriage!

https://marriedandyoung.com

Sean & Lanette Reed

> *"Your baptism in Christ was not just washing you up for a fresh start. It also involved dressing you in an adult faith wardrobe—Christ's life, the fulfillment of God's original promise. Put some clothes on your conduct."*
>
> *Galatians 3:27*

Dress for the Occasion

Dear Stylish Couple,

Have you ever showed up to an event in the wrong attire? Where you thought it was casual but it really turned out to be a black-tie event? Well, we certainly have. And we can tell you, you feel out of place, unprepared, and quite frankly a little embarrassed. Somehow, everyone else got the memo, but you missed it.

Marriage is similar in that there is a special attire required when you connect with your spouse. We have to learn to dress for the occasion. Marriage has a way of exposing what's at the core of your character. We like to define character as

Michael & Alicia Rowntree

> "Be angry and do not sin. Do not let the sun go down on your anger, and do not give the devil a foothold."
>
> Ephesians 4:26–27

Dear Couple Who's Fighting,

On the surface, it would seem that all fighting is bad. But in reality, couples who lack friction lack intimacy. The closer we get, the more candid we become and the more our rough edges *grind*. But if we "play by the rules," those rough edges rub off, and intimacy grows.

One of our rules for dealing with conflict is to address it on the day it arises. This comes from Ephesians 4:26–27: "Be angry and do not sin. Do not let the sun go down on your anger, and do not give the devil a foothold." Do you want to give the devil a foothold in your marriage? Then stuff your anger and hold that grudge. If you do, though, please know that conflict-avoidance comes at the price of "giving

what's etched in your soul. It's what flows from you when you're in the fire. The way you conduct yourself is the clothing, and it flows from your character.

God wants us to put Christlike character on our conduct. "But what about when my spouse does something wrong toward me?" We know what it's like to feel like life is unfair. However, this is something God asks of all of us regardless of the behavior of others. But sadly, some have not spiritually matured to the wardrobe of faith, and they keep showing up to the party with the wrong attire. Even worst, they expect everything to "be normal" even though they're underdressed for marriage.

But if there were one thing we could encourage you to operate in, one set attire to wear every day in your marriage, it would be to allow your character and conduct to be clothed in love.

When you allow love to flow from your heart, you are fulfilling your covenant not because they earn it but also because they need it. Love commits to expressing integrity, grace, trust, and truth to your spouse.

When you're clothed in love, grace is expressed. Grace has a way of recalibrating relationships. In those challenging moments, grace allows you to love your spouse exactly where they are. Looking past the frustrating things they've done to see what's true about them.

When you're clothed in love, trust is given. Trust thrives in an atmosphere of safety and security. They can trust you to be faithful. While sharing vulnerabilities, the relationship is a safe space.

When you are clothed in love, integrity flows from your heart. Your spouse doesn't have to worry about you being a different person in public than you are in private. That regardless of where you are, you are the same morally good person. It's not just what you show people but who you really are. Integrity is when you speak well of them behind their backs, even when they haven't been their best toward you.

And when you're clothed in love, truth follows. It's when you understand the importance of not just sharing the truth, but it's how you share it. The truth is shared with tenderness in a way that your partner will hear it and benefit from it.

Are you dressed in God's best attire for marriage? The best clothing is Christlike living, expressed through your loving conduct toward your spouse.

Love,
Sean and Lanette

About Us

For 12 years, the Reeds have spoken to thou
at marriage conferences, workshops, retreat
With 15 years of pastoral experience Sean
a unique way of presenting truths & practi
couples thrive. Sean & Lanette have over 2
their YouTube videos that provide marri
couples. The Reeds live with their three k
NC, where they're the Marriage and I
Opendoor Church.

https://www.seanandlanette.c

the devil a foothold."

So, how do we deal with our anger? As we saw in Ephesians 4:26, we must allow ourselves to "be angry"—express, don't suppress. We can't get rid of an emotion by pretending we don't feel it! Channeled properly, anger can be used by God to drive us toward true peace and greater intimacy. Channeled improperly, anger explodes like a raging fire, or else it grows cold and unfeeling like frostbitten toes. "Hot anger" is rage, which flares in a moment and *destroys God's blessing*. "Cold anger" is bitterness, which festers over time and *blinds us to God's blessing*. One way we know that the devil has a foothold is that our anger consistently turns hot or cold.

In our culture, people don't want to talk about the devil—it sounds spooky or even childish—but the devil is as real as the anger he manipulates. In the same epistle quoted above, the apostle reminds us of Satan's reality: "Our battle is not against flesh and blood, but...against the spiritual forces of evil in the heavenly realms" (Ephesians 6:12).

Alicia and I learned this lesson poignantly on June 5, 2012. It was our eighth anniversary, and we met for lunch at Ahoyama, our favorite sushi restaurant. As Alicia began chewing, her jaw suddenly fell. Her open palm groped for the side of her face. "I can't feel my cheeks," she said with shock and slurred words. I paid hastily, grabbed her by the hand, and we rushed to the hospital. To make a long story short, they diagnosed her with three maladies, which she still suffers from: Bilateral Bell's Palsy, Sjogren's Syndrome, and glaucoma.

Medically, there's no explanation for these seemingly disparate conditions to occur simultaneously. But spiritually, it makes perfect sense. First of all, we'd recently made a huge decision, as I had accepted the role of senior pastor at Wellspring Church only a few months prior. Second, out of all the times this could have happened, it was on our literal anniversary date, as if the devil was making a symbolic statement: *"I'm coming after your marriage."*

Countless marriage books teach us how to be better partners, but few prepare us for the "spiritual battlefield" of holy matrimony. Think about it: the devil's first assault was on the world's first marriage—a tragic scene that ended in fingers being pointed and intimacy breaking down (Genesis 3). Marriage skills are not enough to succeed in marriage. We have to know how to fight, which means that we must know who our true enemy is.

After this experience, Alicia and I made significant changes in our prayer life because prayer is how we win the spiritual battle (Ephesians 6:18). We started a prayer calendar, where we each shared prayer requests with a different friend, each day of the week. We also began spending more time praying together each day. I'm not going to say that marriage became a cakewalk after that, but ever since we learned to fight the spiritual battle, "battles" in marriage became less heated. Rather than being controlled by our anger, more with each year, we are led by God's Spirit.

So, couple that's fighting, our encouragement to you is this: deal with your anger on the day it arises, and give your days more fully to prayer. Fights will inevitably happen, but as long as you know who your true enemy is, you'll be far less likely to turn your partner into one. Rather, you'll enjoy each other as friends and lovers, and marriage will flourish like the garden it was originally designed for.

Sincerely,
Michael and Alicia

About Us

Michael Rowntree has been a pastor at Wellspring since 2005, the year after he married Alicia Rowntree. Together, they have four kids: Anna, Hudson, Will, and Molly. Michael speaks Spanish, rides a motorcycle, plays the djembe, and laughs at everything (especially his own jokes).

https://wellspringdfw.org/staff-michael-rowntree/

Scott & Leah Silverii

> *"But we all, with open face beholding as in a glass the glory of the Lord, are changed into the same image from glory to glory, even as by the Spirit of the Lord"*
>
> *2 Corinthians 3:18*

Dear Couple in Transition,

We've been there! Some of you might be wondering what it is to be a couple in transition, or that it might not apply to you at all, but we can assure you, at some point (many points) during your marriage, you'll be going through a transition.

Have you just had a baby? Have you experienced the loss of a parent? Bought a new house? Moved? Gotten a new job or retired? Are you empty nesters? These are all periods of transition and they can be HARD. They can put strain on a marriage like nothing else can.

Philippians 4: 6–7 says: "Do not be anxious about anything, but in everything by prayer and supplication with thanksgiving let your requests be made known to God. And the peace of God, which surpasses all understanding, will guard your hearts and your minds in Christ Jesus."

Scott and I know about transition. We're a blended family of seven from two different states and two very different backgrounds. Within the first year of our marriage we'd sold two houses, built a new home, Scott retired from law enforcement, his father passed away, and we decided we didn't want to live in the state we were building our house, so we sold it and moved to Texas. It was the craziest and most hectic time of our lives. We were just trying to hold on to our marriage by the end of that first year. And it was only by the grace of God that we did.

There are moments in our lives when things are so hard we wonder if we are being punished. What did I do to make God so angry? What did my spouse do? But the truth is, God loves us, and He's not punishing us. Sometimes our seasons of transition are no fault of our own, and sometimes seasons of transition are caused by our own sin or the choices we make.

Often, your season of transition is actually God preparing you to be moved into the next season of your life. The Bible talks about moving from glory to glory and in those movements there are obvious times where there appears to be an absence of glory. Those are the transitional periods of transformation.

These seemingly dark times are also the perfect

opportunities to draw closer to Christ and each other in the precise way God designed your relationship to function. Accepting the reality that tough times will come helps to soften the blow when shielded by the comfort of God's loving promises.

Gaining the spiritual maturity as a couple to accept the tough times in transition as a preparation for new beginnings will also help you both in drawing together in God's light as opposed to stumbling apart in the dark. We want to encourage you to seek peace and sincerely trust God in the most difficult depths of those life transitions. We understand that it may be challenging to expect a sense of peace amidst the chaos of the unknown and trying times, but God's peace is not dependent upon an absence of chaos—it is your Rock in the middle of your storm.

When you feel lost in transition, make the commitment to stop where you are, linger in God's presence, and cling to the Rock of salvation and each other until the light of Christ again shines its way along your new life path. Holding tight to each other through the storms and keeping your eyes focused on Christ will get you through them faster and with the peace that passes all understanding. Each transition will bond you tighter than you could ever imagine and deepen your love.

All our Love,
Scott and Leah

About Us

Dr. Scott and Leah Silverii have a blended family of seven kids, a French Bulldog named Bacon, and a micro-mini Goldendoodle named Biscuit. They founded *Blue Marriage,* a first responders ministry to help America's heroes ensure their relationship at home is safe while they are out protecting us.

Scott, a retired chief of police, holds a PhD in cultural anthropology and is working towards his Doctor of Ministry at The King's University. He is a nationally renowned speaker and author of over forty books. Leah, a dynamic presenter, is a *New York Times* and *USA Today* bestselling author of over sixty titles.

https://www.silveriiministry.com

Dave & Rebekah Stotts

> "Like arrows in the hand of a warrior are the children of one's youth. Blessed is the man who fills his quiver with them!"
>
> *Psalm 127:4–5*

Dear Weary Parents,

There is good news and bad news. First the good. God loves marriage and has created the most effective incubator for the love of a man and woman to flourish and for His kingdom to expand. Marriage is great! Now the bad: it will almost never feel that way! Okay, that's a bit of an exaggeration, it will *sometimes* feel that way. But when it doesn't, it's critical to remember that God is there in the midst of your marriage and family even when (and *especially* when) it feels like a struggle. The struggle is part of His plan.

It's often true that opposites attract, and Rebekah and I are very different. Different interests, different priorities, different ways of dealing with stress. But we saw in each other the most important thing two people can share—a commitment to Christ and a desire to grow His Kingdom with a family. A marriage can thrive no matter how differently the spouses are wired if they share that commitment. On the other hand, two spouses exactly alike can doom their marriage if they don't share that commitment.

Jesus said: "Seek first the kingdom of God and his righteousness, and all these things will be added to you" (Matthew 6:33). If a husband and wife's focal point is Christ, their interests are perfectly aligned no matter what. Opposites may attract for a while, but for a marriage to endure, those spouses have to first and foremost be attracted to Christ. That is the spiritual glue that holds them together for life.

Of course the other adhesive for marriage is children. God loves them and wants a lot of them! Why else would God make the one act that results in creating new humans also be the act that is the most enjoyable thing a husband and wife can do together? Follow the logic: God delights in big families. "Be fruitful and multiply," God tells Adam and Eve. Psalm 127 tells us that children are a reward and "like arrows in the hand of a warrior are the children of one's youth. Blessed is the man who fills his quiver with them!"

(Psalm 127:4–5)

But there is more bad news. Everything in our culture is set up to make this fail. We are bombarded with seductive daily messages to live for our own self-interest and personal fulfillment. The world promises happiness so long as our own personal desires are pursued. But any honest person can tell you that's an empty promise and a pernicious lie. That kind of happiness is fleeting and fickle. A person may successfully climb the ladder of self-interest and personal gain, but at the end of the day, it will just be them at the top. Alone.

When a Christ-focused man and woman say, "I do," it is nothing less than a declaration of war against those lies. And war is hard. Pouring out your life for your spouse and kids, sometimes without so much as a "thank you," will wear you out emotionally, physically, even spiritually. But Rebekah and I often remind each other, God sees even when no one else does. And His rewards aren't always immediately realized. The work in a marriage and family is an investment for future rewards. Rewards far outlasting and outshining anything this shallow world has to offer.

Jesus said, "If anyone would come after me, let him deny himself and take up his cross daily and follow me" (Luke 9:23). There are many profound scripture passages on marriage and family, but in our opinion, none quite so perfect as that one. A durable fulfilling marriage is hard, but nothing worth pursuing isn't. So be encouraged. The weariness you feel is part of God's plan to conform you more into the image of His Son. In a way, a wedding is also a funeral, for you die to yourself that day. Only to discover God's wonderful plan to awaken you to deeper and more lasting blessings you never knew were possible.

Love,
Dave and Rebekah

About Us

Dave Stotts, host and editor of Drive Thru History, has 12 years working in Christian media production. His work has taken him to 27 countries to shoot and edit award-winning documentaries. Dave lives in Dallas, Texas, with his wife, Rebekah, and their two sons.

https://drivethruhistory.com

Larry & Devi Titus

> "Complete my joy by being of the same mind, having the same love, being in full accord and of one mind. Do nothing from selfish ambition or conceit, but in humility count others more significant than yourselves"
>
> Philippians 2:2–3

Dear Loving Couples,

Devi and I have been married for fifty-six years. I can count the times we have had a fight on both hands, or maybe just one. We just don't fight. It's true.

I'm sure there are a number of reasons: the stability of the families we came from, the honor we saw our parents bestowing on one another, and even the fact that in neither family was there shouting, screaming, demeaning words, or uncontrolled anger. We both had excellent examples.

There is one other major reason, however, maybe the most important—we work as one. Each of us knows the areas where we are weak and strong.

We know where our spouse excels. I know when I need to prefer her, and she knows when to honor me. I know when it's time to decrease so she may be elevated, and she knows when to decrease so I can initiate. I love to see Devi promoted and she loves to see me honored. It has worked great for fifty-six years. We are a symphony of harmonies.

There are times Devi is in the driver's seat, and there are times when I am. I'm just as comfortable being in the passenger seat, letting her drive, figuratively speaking. It's the same for her. (Of course, those rules don't apply when it's time to find a parking place). I'm not intimidated by her gifts and she is not suppressed by mine. We work as a unit. We love symphonies more than solos. We love to be together, work together, drive together, eat together, socialize together, recreate together, and go to bed together.

Many couples live their entire lives without ever coming into unity. I can't think of a greater tragedy. They operate as two separate people in two separate worlds, never becoming one, as God intended from the beginning. They are married legally but not physically or spiritually. If it weren't for sex they never would come together. And, unfortunately, in many marriages they are not unified in that either.

Many marriages do not look like the godhead, where the persons of God, though individual, operate in total unity, with each honoring and submitting to the other. God's mandate that the "two should become one" is more than a good idea. It's a requirement for a healthy marriage.

Our English word, *symphony*, comes from the Greek word *sumphoneo*. It means to speak the same thing at the same time, yet with different voices. Jesus uses it in Matthew 18:19: "Again, I say to you, if two of you agree on earth about anything they ask, it will be done for them by my Father in heaven" (ESV). There is no life area where unity is more important than in marriage. Can you imagine how blessed a marriage could be if couples would live and work in unity?

For those who complain, "But my spouse is different from me," I respond, "That's what makes a good marriage." Diversity is necessary to produce harmony. You should be praising God for your diversity, not complaining. If you both sounded and thought the same, it would be a solo. Solos are beautiful, but without background harmonies they eventually becoming boring and monotonous. If everyone were to sing melody there would be no diversity, no harmony. I contend that harmony is more beautiful than a single melody, and a symphony is more beautiful than a solo.

Your goal should be to make your marriage a symphony, not a solo. And this can only be accomplished if you choose to prefer one another. Paul said in Philippians 2:2–3: "Complete my joy by being of the same mind, having the same love, being in full accord and of one mind. Do nothing from selfish ambition or conceit, but in humility count others more significant than yourselves" (ESV). These verses also have several "symphony words" in them: "same mind," "one mind." If you build your marriage on selflessness, rather than selfishness, you will see the spirit in your marriage begin to turn around. Then, unity will be right around the corner. I can begin to hear the strains of the symphony already. It's time you start making music together.

Love,
Larry and Devi

About Us

Larry Titus has served over 38 years in effective and innovative pastoral ministry. He has been in ministry more than 55 years. He is president of Kingdom Global Ministries, a missions and mentoring organization he founded in 1992. Larry and his wife, Devi, live in Colleyville, TX. They have two children, Trina Titus Lozano and Dr. Aaron P. Titus, six grandchildren, and eleven great-grandchildren.

https://www.kingdomglobal.com

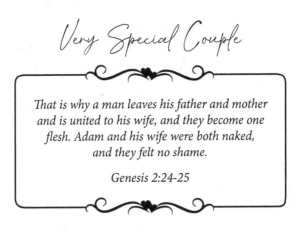

Very Special Couple

*That is why a man leaves his father and mother
and is united to his wife, and they become one
flesh. Adam and his wife were both naked,
and they felt no shame.*

Genesis 2:24-25

Dear Couple Who Holds All Potential,

You are the authors of your very own marriage. We've all loved sharing our thoughts, dreams and prayers with you, but every moment of every day, you have the wonderful opportunity to write what your marriage story will read.

We want you both to take the time to reflect on the last twenty-seven days and in all that was shared with you. Receive what applies and allow it to bless your relationship. Now is the most important and special of these last days. Today is when our very special author couple gets to share their hearts with each other.

Each of your marriage champion couples have held nothing back. We've all committed to writing this devotional as a way to encourage and bless you. Now, our prayer is that you will give each other the very same effort of honesty, vulnerability and love. Hold nothing back because there is nothing without holding each other.

Become one, as Genesis 2:24 so beautifully illustrates. Your marriage is unique, special and was created by God our Father to thrive. There is a 100% chance of growing an incredible covenant relationship when God is placed and remains at the center.

Love, cherish, honor and adore one another and enjoy this powerful opportunity to be the author of your very own love story.

From Love's Letters

9 781951 129408